hand-made habitats

POND

Paul Wright

Photographs by Robert Pickett

A & C Black · London

First published 1992
A & C Black (Publishers) Limited
35 Bedford Row, London WC1R 4JH

ISBN 0-7136-3551-7

A CIP catalogue record for this book
is available from the British Library.

Acknowledgements

Illustrations by Patricia Newell of John Martin and
Artists Limited.

Photographs by Robert Pickett, except for: p5b and p28
Jenny Matthews; p25 Clive Druett, Papillio; pp26/27
Jamie Harron, Papillio and p27t Robert Smith, Papillio.

The author and publisher would like to thank the staff and
pupils of Bolshaw Primary School, Bredbury Green Junior
School, Lum Head Primary School and Eardley Junior
School whose help and co-operation made this book possible.

Filmset by Rowland Phototypesetting Limited,
Bury St Edmunds, Suffolk
Printed in Italy by Imago

Contents

A pond habitat   4

Make an indoor pond habitat   6

Make a mini-pond outdoors   8

Planning a full-size pond   10

Digging and lining your pond   14

Stocking your pond   16

Preparation for pond-dipping   18

Dipping a pond   22

Identifying your catch   24

Pond-watching through the year   26

Surveying a pond   28

Reclaiming a pond   30

Index, identification guides and useful addresses   32

A pond habitat

Have you ever looked carefully into a pond in spring? If you have, you will know that ponds provide a habitat for thousands of different creatures. All these creatures compete for survival by hunting, eating, fighting and mating.

The plants and animals in a pond make up an ecosystem, which has to be kept in a delicate balance, like the larger world that we live in.

Great Diving Beetle larva ▼

The ecosystem works like this. The pond's fierce carnivores, or flesh-eaters, like the Great Diving Beetles and Water Scorpions, prey on the more plentiful plant-eating herbivores, such as daphnia, freshwater shrimps and China Mark Moth larvae. These depend on speed, camouflage or just sheer luck to survive. The plants that provide food for the herbivores need clean water and sunshine to thrive and grow.

The pond is kept clean by scavengers and detrivores such as Mayfly larvae, Bloodworms and Midge larvae. These creatures live by scavenging, eating dead and decaying plants and animals.

If a pond becomes polluted, such as the one in the picture below, the whole ecosystem quickly begins to break down, threatening the survival of all the pond's creatures. This book has ideas for how polluted ponds can be turned back into healthy habitats for pond life.

You may be lucky enough to have a pond in or near your school or home that you can visit and observe. If you haven't got a pond nearby, you can make a mini pond environment quite easily. Many people have even built their own full-size pond and this book will show you how it's done.

Make an indoor pond habitat

Creating a pond habitat indoors is a good way of studying pond creatures close up. It can also give you a clear view of many of the things that happen under the surface of the water.

Use the largest fishtank you can find to build your pond habitat. Ask your friends and relatives – you may find that someone has a tank that they don't use anymore.

Cover the bottom of the tank with sand and gravel. Then add a few larger stones of different sizes. Pour water into the tank until it is three-quarters full. This will give you a better view of the things that happen on the surface of the water.

Fill your tank with pond water if you can, as this will already have a lot of creatures living in it. Make sure that you include some mud from the bottom of the pond. The mud will be rich in nutrients and full of living things. If you do use mud, the water will take a few days to clear.

If you use tap water to fill your tank pond, you must let it stand for a few days before you put anything living into it. Tap water contains chlorine, which can be harmful to living things. The chlorine will disappear in a couple of days.

Next put some pondweed into the tank. Put in enough to half fill the water. This will make sure that the water has enough oxygen in it to keep the creatures healthy. It will also provide food for the herbivores. Water Milfoil, Canadian Pondweed, Hornwort and Starwort are good varieties of pondweed to use. Root the pondweed into the sand and gravel at the bottom of the tank.

After a few days, start to introduce pond creatures into the tank. Think carefully before you do this and use a reference guide to help you. There is a list of useful reference guides on page 32 of this book. What do you think would happen if you introduced fierce predators into such a small system?

Take a good look at the tank every day. You will soon get to know the inhabitants. Keep a record of the activity that you see on the surface and under the water.

Make a mini-pond outdoors

If you'd like to create a pond habitat outdoors, but haven't enough space to build a full-size pond, you could set up a mini-pond. This is very similar to setting up a tank indoors. You can watch the changes that take place each day.

A mini-pond can be any size, from a margarine tub set in the ground to a washing-up bowl or an old baby bath. Use a wide, shallow container with a large surface area. This will allow enough oxygen into the water to keep the pond creatures healthy.

Find a place where your mini-pond won't be disturbed too much, away from direct sunlight. Dig a hole and set the container into the ground so that it can't be knocked over.

Put some sand and gravel on the bottom of the mini-pond. This gives the creatures that live on the bottom somewhere to hide and the pondweed something to grow in. Put some larger stones on top of the sand and gravel.

Next, add the water and then the pondweed as if you were building a fishtank pond indoors.

Once you've set up your mini-pond you can check on its progress every day. In the spring and summer it won't be very long before you will spot some insects beginning to appear in the water. There'll be less to see in the winter when most pondlife either dies or hibernates.

You could hurry things up a little by using water and a little mud from an established pond. This will already have lots of creatures living in it. You will need a magnifying glass to see most of them.

Eventually the pond will develop an ecosystem of its own without any help. The system that develops will be perfect for a pond of this size. The bigger the pond, the more life and variety you will see.

Planning a full-size pond

Building a full-size pond from scratch is an exciting thing to do. But a project like this needs a lot of careful planning.

First of all you will need to find a suitable place to build a pond. This could be an area of your garden at home or a playing field or patch of waste land within your school grounds. Raised ponds made of bricks or concrete can be built on a paved or concrete-covered area.

Once you've picked a suitable site you will need to check that there are no pipes and drains running underneath it. If possible, look at a plan of your chosen site. This will show you the areas to avoid.

Before you start to plan your pond, make a list of all the things you'll need to think about.

Have you got enough space for a full-size pond? The surface area needs to be at least three square metres.

Will the pond be safely away from young children?

Are there any trees at your chosen site? Falling leaves from overhanging trees can clog up a pond.

What materials will you use to build the pond? Sometimes ponds are made of concrete. But concrete can crack and be difficult to repair. Many old ponds and canals were made with a special clay called bentonite, but this is very heavy and difficult to transport.

Often a pondliner made of butyl rubber is the most suitable material to use. This is very tough and is sold at garden centres. You can buy cheaper pondliners, but they don't last as long.

How will you pay for the materials? If you're building a pond at school, you could think about applying for a grant for your pond. There is a list of addresses to write to for more information on page 32.

Once you've chosen a suitable site and investigated which materials to use, think about the pond itself.

Will you be able to investigate the pond safely? You will need to plan for some dipping platforms. These are shallow shelves around the inside edge of the pond where you can stand safely.

Plan to have different zones in your pond. Part of it needs to be at least one metre deep to stop the pond freezing up in winter. The edges of the pond can be shallower – say ten centimetres deep. These shallower edges make safe dipping platforms and provide good shelter for shallow water plants and animals.

Can you design your pond so that it will be difficult to vandalise?

Choose a place that is quiet and unlikely to be disturbed.

Keep fences low. Vandals do not usually bother to damage a fence that they can climb over easily.

Use nettles, thistles and thorny plants to keep vandals away from the pond itself.

Use bark chippings rather than logs to make a wood pile at the edge of the pond. They will attract just as many animals but are less likely to be thrown into the pond or through a window.

Use gravel instead of a stone pile to attract minibeasts. Gravel will cause less damage than stones if it is thrown around.

Keep the pond area free of litter — don't let your pond look like a vandalised area.

Who will look after the pond in the future? If you plan it carefully, it won't need very much maintenance.

If vandalism is likely to be a serious problem, you could think about creating a marshy area instead of a pond.

Digging and lining your pond

Before you start to dig out the shape of your pond, mark the outline carefully with string. You'll need as much help with the digging as possible, so collect together as many people as you can.

Once the shape has been dug out, look closely to make sure that there are no sharp stones or roots sticking up which could puncture the pond liner and cause leaks. Use sand, newspaper or pieces of old carpet to line the hole and make a smooth surface for the butyl liner to cover.

Unfold the butyl liner, being careful not to stretch or puncture it. Gently lower it into the hole so that it overlaps the sides of the pond.

Filling a full-size pond with water can take a long time, especially if you are using buckets to carry the water from a tap. You could use a hosepipe if you can find one long enough to stretch from the tap to the pond.

Once the pond is full of water, anchor the edges of the butyl liner down with pieces of turf. Then use a pair of scissors to trim away any of the liner that is not forming part of the pond. The weight of water in the fully-filled pond will help to keep the rest of the liner in place.

Remember to let the water in the pond stand for a few days to allow the chlorine to evaporate. Then you will be ready to start introducing first of all, plants, and then pond creatures into your pond.

Stocking your pond

When you are stocking the pond, try to include several different kinds of plants.

Floating plants look attractive and they provide shelter and support for other living things.

Floating plants include:

Water Lilies (1)
Broad-leaved Pondweed (2)
Water Crowfoot
Water Soldier
Frogbit
Lesser Duckweed
Ivy-leaved Duckweed

Choose plants for the edges of the pond that will attract birds as well as pondlife.

Pond edge plants include:

Yellow Iris (3)
Flowering Rush (4)
Reedmace
Branched Burreed
Water Plantain
Great Willowherb
Common Reed
Purple Bogbean

Other plants live under the water. They keep the oxygen in the water at a healthy level.

Underwater plants include:

Water Milfoil (5)
Starwort
Hornwort

You need to be very careful about the plants and animals that you introduce to your pond as some things could damage its delicate ecosystem. Here are some things to avoid:

Canadian Pondweed

This is suitable for indoor tank ponds, but outdoors in Britain, this foreign plant will soon choke your pond up and be very difficult to get rid of.

Try to avoid plants that don't come from the same country as your pond. British plants have evolved to fit into British ponds perfectly, just as Canadian plants fit into Canadian ponds and so on.

Fish

Unless your pond is quite big and well established, its ecosystem will break down if fish are added. They would just eat most of the other creatures in the pond.

Expensive plants

If you ask around you're almost sure to find someone who will let you have a few plants for free from an established pond.

If you do, ask them for some of the 'matting' which is formed by the roots of the taller plants. This contains all sorts of animals, nutrients and seeds that will soon get your pond springing into life.

Remember: you are not allowed to remove plants and animals from the wild without the permission of the landowner.

Preparation for pond-dipping

Before you begin to investigate the pond you have built, you will need to collect together some pieces of equipment. You can make most of the equipment yourself from everyday materials. It needn't cost very much and it will help you to make the most of your investigations.

A pond dipper's kit

Empty margarine tubs with lids – these are good to use for viewing your catch. The white plastic makes it easy to see the pondlife. The lid is useful if you decide to take something into the classroom to put into your tank.

White plastic spoons – these are useful for picking up and viewing pondlife without damaging it.

Pooters – these are ideal for catching and viewing creatures on the pond's surface.

Make your own pooter

You will need:

two short pieces of plastic tubing

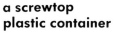

a screwtop plastic container

a rubber band

a gimlet

plasticine

a piece of material (net curtain fabric or a nylon stocking will do)

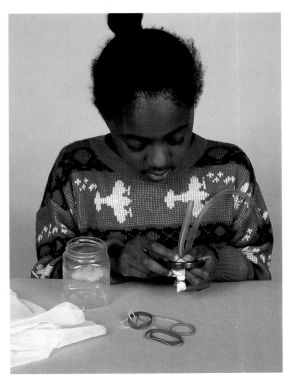

Use a gimlet to make two small holes in the top of the plastic container. Push two short pieces of plastic tubing through the holes and seal the gap with plasticine.

Use the rubber band to hold the piece of material over the end of one tube. This acts as a filter to stop anything being sucked into your mouth. Then screw the lid back on to the container.

To use the pooter, point the end of one tube at the insect and suck through the other tube.

Make your own dipping net

A fine-meshed net with a long handle is essential for pond dipping and useful for investigating the mud at the bottom of the pond.

You will need: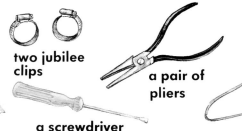

two jubilee clips

a pair of pliers

a wire coat hanger

a screwdriver

a needle and thread

a piece of nylon curtain netting about 60cm by 30cm

a broomhandle

Fold and hem along one 60cm edge of the curtain netting. Fold the netting in half, and make it into a bag by sewing along the bottom and up the side. Make sure that the hem runs around the top of the bag.

Straighten the coat hanger out with the pliers and bend it into a loop (you may need an adult's help to do this). Gently thread the hem at the top of the bag around the loop. Clamp the ends of the wire firmly to the broom handle with the jubilee clips.

Make your own pond trap

You will need:

 string

some stones

a plastic lemonade bottle without its lid

scissors

Cut around the bottle just below the slope of the neck. Add some stones to the bottom of the bottle. These will help to weigh it down when it is underwater. Turn the top of the bottle around and push it firmly into the base. Tie a piece of string around the bottle to use as a handle.

Lower the trap gently into the water and suspend it at your chosen depth for a day or two. Then carefully lift it out and observe and record your catch. Return the creatures to the pond immediately after you've finished studying them.

Remember, although ponds are exciting places, they can be dangerous. Always follow these commonsense rules:
- Never visit the pond on your own. Take an adult with you every time.
- Make sure that you are dressed warmly.
- When you dip the pond, stand on a dipping platform or in a safe place on the edge of the pond where the ground beneath your feet is flat and firm. Don't dip at steep banksides where it's slippery.
- Wash your hands after visiting the pond.

Dipping a pond

Whatever size pond you build, good pond-dipping starts a long way from the pond itself. Approach the pond slowly and quietly – otherwise you will frighten away most of the pondlife even before you reach the water's edge.

When you arrive at the pond, stand still or sit down for a few minutes. What can you hear? Perhaps dragonflies humming as they hover over the water, or a frog plopping into the pond.

Pondskater ▲   **Water Fleas** ▼

Watch the surface of the water. What can you see? Many creatures such as Pond Skaters and Water Boatmen live on the surface. Others such as the Great Diving Beetle and the Wolf Spider come to the surface for air.

Look into the water. You'll notice different creatures at different depths. Swimmers like the Cyclops and the Water Flea will be invisible from the edge of the pond. But you'll be able to spot snails and other creatures on plant stems and underneath leaves.

Gently fill a container with water. Slide your net into the pond and make a slow, smooth stroke through the water. Turn your net inside out and rinse it in the container.

Look carefully. Many of the pond creatures are difficult to see at first. Some are transparent, some are very small. If possible, use a hand lens to examine the water.

If you catch something larger that you want to examine more closely, use a pooter or a spoon to transfer it carefully to a container of water with a lid. If you plan to study an air-breathing creature that you find above the water, wrap it gently in wet weed.

Repeat the dip, smoothly and gently. Take care not to stir up the bottom of the pond yet.

Now try dipping along the stems of the plants. Be careful not to damage them. Dip your net into the mud at the bottom of the pond. On the surface of the pond, wash away the silt and mud and rinse your net into the container again. Make a note of where you dipped each time.

Identifying your catch

Now you are ready to identify your catch. Look closely at the water in your container. If you are using a transparent container hold it up to the light or put it against a piece of white paper. This will help you to see the creatures more clearly.

Can you spot any? At first they will be quite difficult to see. Most of them will be very tiny and the bodies of some will be almost completely clear.

Concentrate on one creature at a time. If it keeps moving around, put it into a small container by itself. Remember, pond creatures are fragile, so do this very carefully using a teaspoon or a small paintbrush.

What can you see? Try drawing the creature larger than life. This will help when it comes to identifying it. It will be easier if you use a 1cm grid. Put this under the transparent container. Can you use the grid to help you to work out the length of the creature?

Start off by drawing the creature on a piece of paper about 1cm × 2cm. Draw it as large as possible – try to fill the paper.

Copy your picture onto larger pieces of paper, the first one 4cm × 2cm, the second one 8cm × 4cm and the third one 16cm × 8cm. Try to fill the paper each time.

Before you begin identifying your creature, ask yourself questions like these:

Water Boatman ▼

Where did you catch it? (On the surface, under the surface, on the bottom, or on a plant?)

How long is it?

Is the body divided into sections?

How many sections does it have?

What colour is it?

How many pairs of legs does it have?

Has it got a shell?

Has it got a case?

Has it got a hard case split down the middle?

Once you have recorded your evidence you will need to refer to a good identification guide or 'key'. There are books, computer databases, charts and posters which will help you to identify your creature by asking you questions about it. There is a list of identification guides and keys on page 32.

After you have identified your findings, carefully return everything you've caught to the pond.

Pond-watching through the year

Ponds are changing all the time, with the weather, with the seasons and just by getting older. A pond that teems with life in springtime might seem dead and cold in the winter.

You could survey the same pond at different times of the year, perhaps during the last week of each school term. This will give you an idea of how the pond keeps changing.